BEARDED DRAGONS

by Imogen Kingsley

AMICUS | AMICUS INK

Amicus High Interest and Amicus Ink are published by Amicus
P.O. Box 1329, Mankato, MN 56002
www.amicuspublishing.us

Copyright © 2019 Amicus. International copyright reserved in all countries. No part of this book may be reproduced in any form without written permission from the publisher.

Library of Congress Cataloging-in-Publication Data
Names: Kingsley, Imogen, author.
Title: Bearded dragons / by Imogen Kingsley.
Description: Mankato, Minnesota : Amicus/Amicus Ink, [2019] | Series: Lizards in the wild | Audience: K to Grade 3. | Includes index.
Identifiers: LCCN 2018002407 (print) | LCCN 2018006673 (ebook) | ISBN 9781681515922 (pdf) | ISBN 9781681515540 (library binding) | ISBN 9781681523927 (paperback)
Subjects: LCSH: Bearded dragons (Reptiles)--Juvenile literature.
Classification: LCC QL666.L223 (ebook) | LCC QL666.L223 K56 2019 (print) | DDC 597.95/5--dc23
LC record available at https://lccn.loc.gov/2018002407

Photo Credits: Alamy/Vicki Beaver, cover, Michelle Gilders, 2, 22, Rimmi, 10, David Hancock, 17, Mark Higgins, 18; Getty/Arterra, 5, Auscape, 20–21; WikiCommons/Matt Clancy Wildlife Photography, 6; Dreamstime/Stephen Bonk, 9; Flickr/Tambako The Jaguar, 12–13; iStock/CraigRJD, 14

Editor: Mary Ellen Klukow
Designer: Peggie Carley
Photo Researcher: Holly Young

Printed in United States of America

HC 10 9 8 7 6 5 4 3 2
PB 10 9 8 7 6 5 4 3 2 1

TABLE OF CONTENTS

A Desert Dweller	4
A Scaly Body	7
Changing Color	8
Not Picky	11
A Long Tongue	12
A Fast Runner	15
A Big Beard	16
A Head Bobber	19
New Beardies	20
A Look at a Bearded Dragon	22
Words to Know	23
Learn More	24
Index	24

A Desert Dweller

A bearded dragon runs up a post. It is hot and dry. There is not much food. There is not much rain. That is okay. This lizard thrives in the desert.

Check This Out
Bearded dragons are sometimes called beardies. Beardies are **native** to Australia.

A SCALY BODY

A beardie has hard, thin scales. They protect its body. The scales also help keep in **moisture.** This helps beardies live in the dry desert.

> **Check This Out**
> As a beardie grows, its skin gets too small. When the new skin is ready, it sheds the old skin.

CHANGING COLOR

A bearded dragon can change color. If the weather is hot, its scales get lighter. This helps it stay cool. If the weather is cold, its scales get darker. This helps the beardie stay warm.

NOT PICKY

A bearded dragon is an **omnivore**. It eats plants and animals. It is not picky. It will eat anything it can find. It often eats ants and fruit.

A LONG TONGUE

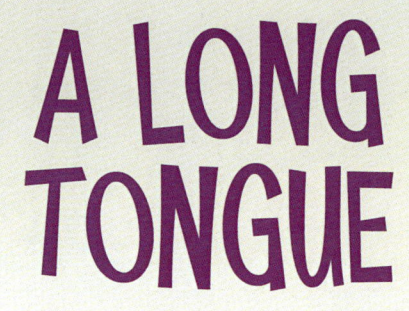

A beetle runs by. The beardie's mouth opens fast. His tongue darts out. It is long. It is sticky. It grabs the bug. Yum!

A FAST RUNNER

A bearded dragon sees a **dingo**. The lizard does not want to be eaten. It runs away fast. It can run 25 miles per hour (40 km/h)!

A BIG BEARD

A beardie rests in a tree. A snake comes. It wants to eat the lizard. The lizard puffs up its **dewlap**. It looks like a big beard. It scares the snake. The beardie is safe.

Check This Out
The inside of the beardie's mouth is brightly colored. Beardies also open their mouths to surprise enemies.

A HEAD BOBBER

Beardies use **body language**. One lizard bobs its head. This means "I am powerful." Another lizard waves its arm. This means "I agree. I do not want to fight."

NEW BEARDIES

A female digs a hole. She lays up to 30 eggs. Then she leaves. The eggs hatch in 75 to 80 days. Soon new beardies will be running through the desert.

A LOOK AT A BEARDED DRAGON

WORDS TO KNOW

body language To use body movements to show other animals how it feels.

dewlap A flap of skin that hangs under the jaw of an animal.

dingo A wild dog that lives in Australia.

moisture Small bits of water and dampness.

native An animal or plant that originally lived or grew in a certain place.

omnivore An animal that eats both plants and animals.

LEARN MORE

Books

Collard, Sneed B. III. *Sneed B. Collard III's Most Fun Book Ever About Lizards*. Watertown, Mass.: Charlesbridge, 2012.

Mara, Will. *Bearded Dragons*. North Mankato, Minn.: Capstone, 2017.

Websites

The Australian Museum: The Bearded Dragon
https://australianmuseum.net.au/central-bearded-dragon

DK Find Out!: Lizards
https://www.dkfindout.com/us/animals-and-nature/reptiles/lizards/

National Geographic: Bearded Dragons
http://natgeo.petsmart.com/bearded-dragon/

INDEX

ants, 11
Australia, 4

beetles, 12
body language, 19

colors, 8, 16

desert, 4, 7, 20
dewlap, 16
dingos, 15

eggs, 20

head bobbing, 19

omnivore, 11

scales, 7, 8
skin, 7
snake, 16

tongue, 12

Every effort has been made to ensure that these websites are appropriate for children. However, because of the nature of the Internet, it is impossible to guarantee that these sites will remain active indefinitely or that their contents will not be altered.